animals

This edition published by Fog City Press
Conceived and produced by Weldon Owen Pty Ltd
61 Victoria Street, McMahons Point
Sydney, NSW 2060, Australia

Copyright © 2008 Weldon Owen Pty Ltd

Group Chief Executive Officer John Owen
President and Chief Executive Officer Terry Newell
Publisher Sheena Coupe
Creative Director Sue Burk
Vice President, International Sales Stuart Laurence
Vice President, Sales and New Business Development Amy Kaneko
Vice President, Sales: Asia and Latin America Dawn Low
Administrator, International Sales Kristine Ravn
Publishing Coordinator Mike Crowton

Consultant Editor Denise Ryan
Managing Editor Jessica Cox
Editor Helen Flint
Designer Gabrielle Green

ISBN: 978-1-74089-662-7

Color reproduction by SC (Sang Choy) International Pte Ltd
Printed by SNP Leefung Printers Ltd
Manufactured in China

10 9 8 7 6 5 4 3 2 1

A WELDON OWEN PRODUCTION

my first

encyclopedia of
animals

Denise Ryan

FOG CITY PRES

Scarlet macaws

Monitor lizard

contents

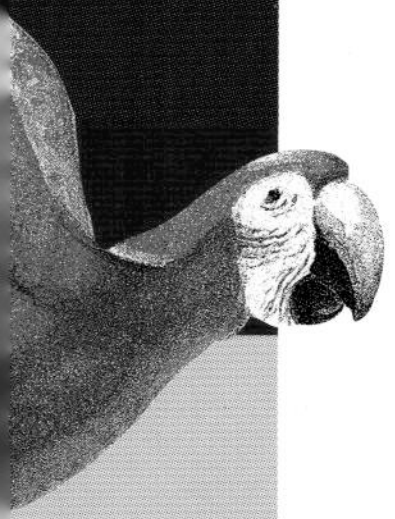

Frog

6 What is an animal?

8 Kangaroos

10 Monkeys

12 Apes

14 Wolves

16 Bears

18 Lions

20 Tigers

22 Elephants

24 Rhinos

26 Whales

28 Jungle birds

30 Eagles

32 Owls

34 Crocodiles

36 Lizards

38 Snakes

40 Frogs

42 Sharks

44 Bugs

46 Glossary

48 Index

What is an animal?

Spiders, frogs, birds, and bears are all animals. Animals with backbones are called vertebrates. Elephants, bears, birds, sharks, and frogs are vertebrates. Animals without backbones are called invertebrates. Butterflies, ants, spiders, and worms are all invertebrates.

Sulfur-breasted toucan
Toucans belong to the bird group.

Brown bear
Bears belong to the mammal group.

What group?

Many animals are very similar to each other. Others are quite different. Animals that are similar are grouped together and given a group name.

Silvertip

The large, gray silvertip shark is a vertebrate because it has a backbone.

Silvertip shark
Sharks belong to the fish group.

Elephant
Elephants belong to the mammal group.

Tarantula
Tarantulas belong to the spider group.

Strawberry poison dart frog
Frogs belong to the amphibian group.

An elephant's trunk has 150,000 bands of muscle.

Kangaroos

Kangaroos are a kind of animal called marsupials. They live in the deserts and grasslands of Australia, where they eat plants. Kangaroos hop on their strong back legs. All female kangaroos have pouches where their babies shelter and feed on their mother's milk.

Boxing kangaroos
Male kangaroos look like they are boxing when they kick and push each other. The winner of the boxing match mates with a female kangaroo.

A male kangaroo is sometimes called a boomer.

Kangaroos live in family groups called mobs. They usually feed in the evening and rest during the day.

Platypus

Australian neighbors

Kangaroos live only in Australia. Two other animals that live only in Australia are the platypus and the echidna.

Ants

Echidna

Monkeys

There are almost 200 different kinds of monkeys. Monkeys live in Africa, Asia, and Central and South America. Some have tails that can grasp and hold objects. Others can grab objects with their fingers and toes. Monkeys live in family groups and spend most of their time in trees.

Woolly monkey

This woolly monkey uses its tail to grip tree branches. This allows it to collect food with its hands.

Hanging on

South American spider monkeys use their tails to hang onto slender branches as they swing from tree to tree.

Cotton-tops

Cotton-top tamarins live in Central America. They spend most of their lives high in the rain forest trees, eating fruit, leaves, and insects.

Hot bath

Japanese macaques survive cold temperatures by bathing in hot springs.

Apes

The group of animals called apes is made up of orangutans, gorillas, and two kinds of chimpanzees. Orangutans live on the islands of Sumatra and Borneo, Indonesia. Gorillas and chimpanzees are found only in Africa.

Orangutan

The people of Sumatra and Borneo call this gentle red ape *Orang Hutan*, which means "People of the Forest."

Gorilla family

Gorillas live in family groups. Each family is led by a large silverback male. He stands upright, roars, and slaps his chest to warn other males to stay away from his mates and children.

Many apes build nests each night in the tops of trees.

Silverback male

Wolves

Wolves are members of a group called dogs. They have keen sight, hearing, and smell, and have 42 strong, sharp teeth. Wolves are excellent hunters and hunt their prey in packs. They let each other know what is happening by howling loudly.

Wolf pack

A wolf pack is led by an adult male and female. The other members of the pack are their children.

Dinnertime

Wolves slowly sneak up on their victim in single file. When their prey tries to escape, the wolves rush to attack.

Red foxes are also dogs.
They can dig holes,
and often bury food
to eat later.

Bears

What do you picture when you think of a bear? Maybe you see a a fierce brown bear or maybe a polar bear? Many bears live in forests and in the icy Arctic. They all have heavy bodies, long, sharp claws, and huge heads with big teeth.

Meal time

Bears eat plants, insects, honey, as well as meat if they can catch it easily. This brown bear has found a marmot's burrow. If it can catch the marmot, it will eat it.

A polar bear's fur is made up of hollow hairs that trap heat. This helps it live in freezing Arctic areas.

Marmot

FUR PATTERN

The giant panda is mainly white. It has black fur on its ears, eye patches, muzzle, legs, and shoulders. It eats only bamboo.

Sharp
claw

Some bears
spend all winter
in a deep sleep
in their dens.

Lions

Lions are a member of the animal group called cats. They have fur, sharp teeth, and they work together to find food. Lions are the only cats to live in groups, which are called prides. Female lions, called lionesses, usually hunt for the whole pride.

Lioness

Lioness lunch

This lioness leaps quickly to grab its frightened prey, a gazelle. If she catches it, other lionesses and lions will join her for the meal.

A pride of lions

Lion prides usually have 4 to 6 animals, although they can have up to 30 members. The females are nearly always related to each other.

Lions can survive for long periods without water.

Lion cub

Tigers

Tigers are the largest members of the cat group. Tigers live in forests and grasslands of India, Siberia, and southeast Asia. They have powerful jaws filled with large teeth. Striped fur covers their bodies.

Even though lots of cats hate getting wet, tigers love water and are good swimmers.

FUR COAT

Tigers have thick black stripes covering their orange bodies. Male tigers have a ruff of fur around the back of their heads.

Stripy fur

The hunt

This tiger is creeping through tall grass to get close to its prey. When it is close enough, it pounces and catches its dinner.

White tigers are found only in zoos.

Elephants

The elephant is the largest living creature on land. The two kinds, the Indian and African elephants, live in family groups. Elephants are so big that they spend most of their time eating plants to fuel their bodies.

Elephants can make sounds that are too low for humans to hear.

Water, mud, and dust

African elephants stay cool by sucking water into their trunks and spraying it over their bodies. They also coat themselves with mud and dust to protect their skins from sunburn and insects.

Trunk
An elephant's trunk is sensitive enough to pick up a blade of grass.

DIFFERENCES

African elephants have large ears and a sloping forehead. Indian elephants have smaller ears and a domed forehead. Which one is the African elephant?

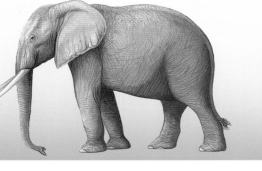

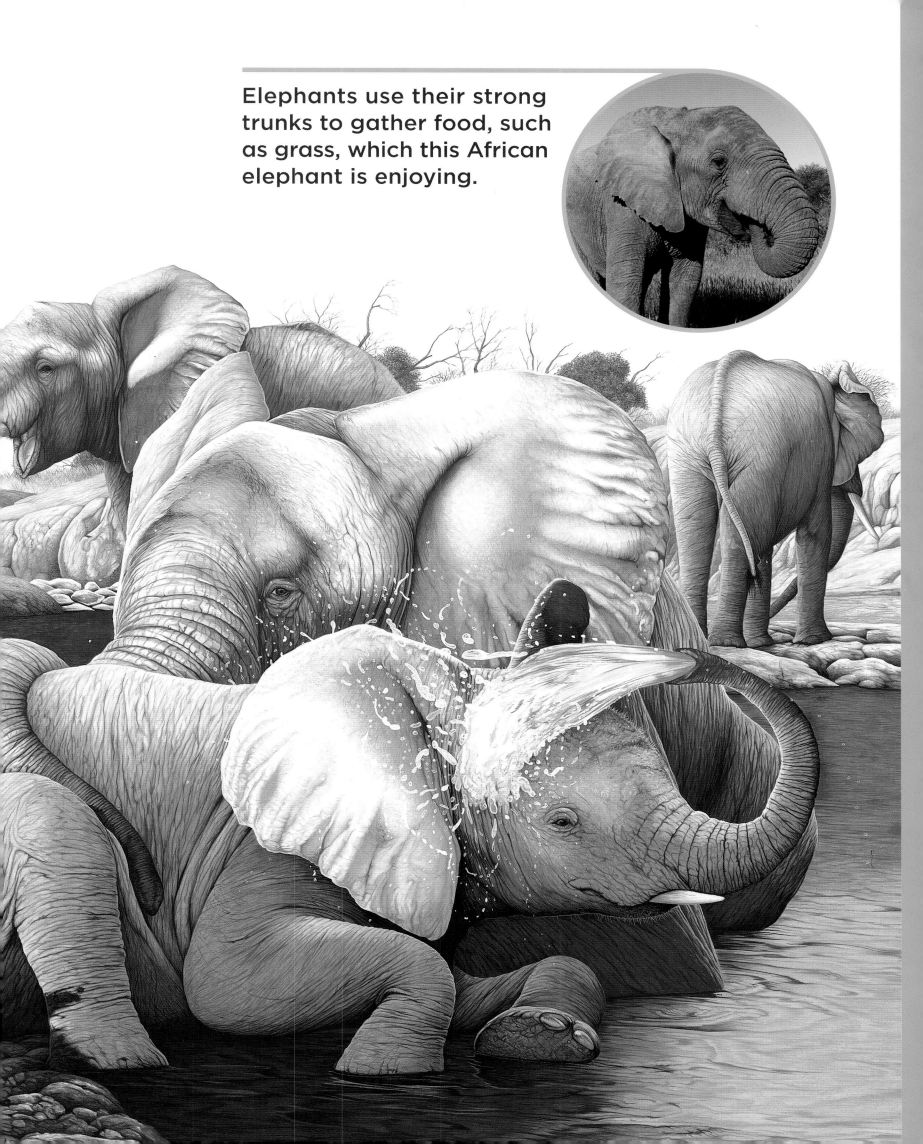

Elephants use their strong trunks to gather food, such as grass, which this African elephant is enjoying.

Rhinos

Rhinoceroses are large animals that live in Asia and Africa. Rhinos eat leaves, buds, shoots, and twigs. They drink freshwater every day, and spend a lot of time wallowing in waterholes to keep themselves cool. They have huge bodies, stumpy legs, and two horns.

Charge!

These spotted hyenas have no chance against a charging rhino. Rhinos usually defend themselves by attacking. They can run quickly when they need to!

Charging rhino

BODY TALK

When their young are under attack, female rhinos form a circle around them. They threaten the attacker with their horns.

Spotted hyena

Humans once hunted rhinos for their horns.

Whales

Whales are large mammals that live in the ocean. They breathe air through blowholes. Their sleek, streamlined bodies move easily through the water. They give birth to calves that can see and swim straight away.

Despite their size, orcas can leap clear out of the water. No one knows exactly why they do it.

DOLPHINS

Dolphins belong to the same group of animals as whales. There are 32 kinds of dolphins. Three of them are below.

Hector's dolphin

Commerson's dolphin

Long-beaked common dolphin

Humpback whales

Humpback whales are a grayish-blue color with light spots. They have stubby dorsal fins and large, thick tails. They feed mainly on krill.

One bowhead whale was thought to have reached 130 years of age.

Jungle birds

Birds have light feathers, strong bones, and powerful flying muscles. A large number of beautiful birds live in the jungle. Most of them spend all their lives among the trees. The birds feed on insects, fruit, and seeds, and build nests high up in the branches.

Toucan

Toucans live in South American rain forests, where they use their colorful bills to pluck fruit, nuts, and berries from trees.

LONG LIFE

Parrots can live for a long time. This black-capped lory can live for more than 40 years.

Bill
A toucan's bill can be as big as its body.

Some toucans have bills almost half as long as their bodies.

Body talk
Scarlet macaws have wide, strong wings that help them to fly quickly. They often fly in pairs or small groups, and call to each other in loud voices.

Eagles

Eagles are some of the largest birds in the world. They can be found everywhere except Antarctica. They belong to a group called birds of prey, or raptors. Eagles are good at flying, have excellent vision, and have strong grasping talons, which makes them great hunters.

Feathered, not bald

Bald eagles are magnificent birds found in North America. They are large birds that have white heads and tails, and are not bald at all.

Spotted harrier

Spotted harriers fly low over fields, swooping down on any mice, frogs, lizards, and snakes they see.

Golden eagles are great hunters. They live in the rocky areas and mountains of North America.

About half of the world's 70,000 bald eagles live in Alaska, USA.

Wing

Owls

Owls sleep during the day and hunt at night. They have talons on their feet for catching prey and hooked beaks for tearing food apart. Their big eyes face forward and their large heads can swivel almost fully around.

A barn owl's eggs hatch after 33 days. The male helps feed the young chicks, which can fly after about 12 weeks.

Caught

Sometimes owls can be spotted hunting during the day, especially when they have young to feed. They mostly hunt small mammals.

Barn owl

The barn owl's large heart-shaped face, white breast, and pale golden wings can make it look quite ghostly at night.

Eye

Barn owls do not hoot. They screech, hiss, snore, and yap.

Crocodiles

Crocodiles and their close relatives, alligators, are large reptiles. They wait for prey to come to the water's edge, then use their strong teeth to drag it underwater. Crocodiles cannot chew, so they tear their food into chunks, which they swallow whole.

If a crocodile's tooth gets knocked out, another grows to take its place.

Hiding out

The alligator hides under the algae on the water's surface.

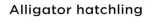

Alligator hatchling

Mother alligator

SNORKEL

Alligators can breathe while they are almost underwater because they have nostrils on the top of their snouts.

Floating
Alligators float with their bodies just below the surface of the water.

Safe place

These alligator hatchlings are being carried to a pond where they will be safe from danger.

Lizards

Lizards have many enemies, such as snakes and birds. Most lizards are able to blend into the background and stay completely still when an enemy approaches. Some lizards have an unusual way of escaping. If they are grabbed by the tail they leave it behind!

Frilly fright

The frill-necked lizard tries to frighten an enemy by pretending to be bigger than it really is. It hisses loudly and opens out the large frill behind its neck.

Frill

Blue-tongued lizard

Small lizards called geckos keep their eyes clean by licking them.

Monitor

Monitor lizards are tropical reptiles with strong bodies and long legs. They can run very fast and give a stinging lash with their tails.

Snakes

There are almost 2,400 kinds of snakes. They come in many different colors and sizes, but they all lay eggs and have scaly skin. Unlike you or me, snakes are cold-blooded. This means they have to lie in the sun, or in warm places, to stay at the correct temperature.

King cobras are the only snakes in the world that build nests for their young.

Waiting for dinner
Carpet pythons are often colored black and yellow. Their patterned skin hides them as they lie in wait for passing prey.

Different snakes have different patterns of scales on their skin.

Spitting cobra

This spitting cobra is spitting venom to defend itself. It can also open out a hood behind its head to make it look bigger than it actually is.

Scaly skin

Frogs

Frogs are amphibians. They spend part of their lives in water and part on land. Frogs lay their eggs in water. The eggs hatch into tadpoles, which lose their tails as they grow. Frogs eat insects, which they catch with their long, sticky tongues.

Frogs can live to between 2 and 40 years old.

Long leg

POISON SKIN

Poison-dart frogs get the poison that covers their skin from the insects they eat. If they are fed other foods, they become harmless.

Poisonous skin

Jump!
Frogs are good jumpers because they have long, powerful back legs, short bodies, and no tail to get in the way.

Warning colors
Poisonous frogs are often small but brightly colored. Their bright colors and patterns warn enemies not to eat them.

Harlequin frog

Corroboree frog

Green tree frogs make loud noises when they call out to other frogs.

Sharks

Sharks are amazing fish that live in every ocean around the world. They have sleek bodies that glide easily through the water. They attack their prey with their sharp teeth. Most sharks do not chew their food. They just gulp it down in large pieces.

Hammerhead sharks are fierce hunters with a good sense of smell for finding their prey.

SHARP AND DEADLY

Shark teeth come in many shapes and sizes. Different teeth are used for catching and eating different food.

Blue shark

Shortfin mako shark

Tiger shark

Great white shark

On the reef

Caribbean reef sharks live in tropical waters near the edge of coral reefs. They are found in the Caribbean Sea.

A shark may have up to 3,000 teeth in its mouth at one time.

Caribbean reef shark

Bugs

Bugs are some of Earth's most common creatures: There are about 1.5 million kinds. Insects, spiders, scorpions, and ants are all called bugs. Bugs do not have backbones but have hard skeletons on the outside of their bodies.

This beautiful butterfly is feeding on nectar from inside flowers.

ATTACK

This spider, called a tarantula, is about to attack a lizard with its powerful fangs.

Tarantula

Lizard

Active and alert

Tiger beetles are fast runners and fliers. They can chase insects easily, and catch them with their strong jaws.

Ants can lift and carry more than 50 times their own weight.

Tiger beetle

Ant

Glossary

Brown bear

Scarlet macaw

amphibians
Animals with a backbone able to live in water and on land

birds
Feathered animals with wings

chimpanzee
An African ape found in tropical forests

continent
A large, unbroken mass of land

coral
Colored substance formed from the skeletons of a tube-shaped animal

dorsal fin
The fin that appears on the back of a whale or a fish

fish
Animals that live in the water, and breathe through gills

flare
To spread or curve outward

invertebrates
Animals without backbones

keratin
A tough protein that forms the outer layer of hair, nails, and horns

krill
Tiny, shrimp-like sea animals

mammals
Animals whose young feed on their mothers' milk

marmot
A small, burrowing rodent

marsupials
A group of mammals in which the mother nurses her young in a pouch

muscles
Tissues made up of fibers which help bodies move

muzzle
The snout of an animal

Orangutan

Long-beaked
common dolphin

pouch
A type of pocket used to carry a marsupial's young

prey
Any animal hunted or killed by another animal

protect
To keep or guard from harm

raptors
Birds of prey that hunt for food using their talons

reefs
A line of coral near the surface of tropical waters

reptiles
Cold-blooded, air-breathing animals

ruff
A ring of differently marked hair around the neck of an animal

species
A group of animals able to breed among themselves

stalk
To approach quietly and secretly

talons
A bird of prey's claws

tropical
The areas of Earth that are near the equator

tuft
A bunch of hair held tightly at the base

venomous
Able to make venom

vertebrates
Animals with a spine or backbone

Index

A

African elephant 22
alligators 34–5
amphibians 40–1
ants 6, 9, 44, 45
apes 12–13
Australian frill-necked lizard 36

B

bald eagle 30
barn owl 32–3
bears 6, 16–17
birds 6, 28–33, 36
black-capped lory 28
black rhinoceros 24, 25
blue shark 42
blue whales 26–7
boomer (kangaroo) 8
bowhead whales 27
brown bear 6, 17
bugs 44–5
butterflies 6, 44

C

Caribbean reef shark 43
carpet python 38
chimpanzees 12
Commerson's dolphin 26
communication 14, 22, 28, 29, 33, 41
corroborree frog 41
cotton-top tamarins 10
crocodiles 34–5

D

defense 24, 36

E

eagles 30–1
echidna 9
eggs 32, 38, 40
elephants 6, 7, 22–3

F

family groups 9, 10, 13, 14, 18, 22
feathers 9, 28, 30
fighting 8, 24
fish 42
food 10, 14, 17, 18, 23, 32, 34, 40, 42
foxes 15
frogs 6, 7, 40–1
fur 9, 16, 18, 20

G

gazelle 18
giant panda 16
golden eagles 30
gorillas 12–13
great white shark 42
green tree frog 41
grouping animals 6

H

hammerhead sharks 42
harlequin frog 41
harrier hawk 30
Hector's dolphin 26
herds (elephants) 22
hibernation 16
hood (cobra) 39
horns 24
hunting 14, 15

I

Indian elephant 22
insects 10, 17, 23, 40, 44–5
invertebrates 6

J

Japanese macaque 11
jungle birds 28–9

K

kangaroos 8–9
keratin 29
king cobra 38
krill 26

L

lions 18–19
lizards 36–7, 44
long-beaked common dolphin 26

M

mammals 18, 26
marsupials 8
mob (kangaroos) 9
monitor lizard 37
monkeys 10–11

O

orangutans 12, 13
orcas 26

P

pack (wolves) 14
platypus 9
poison 38, 39, 40
polar bears 16
pouches 8
pride (lions) 18

R

raptors 30, 32
reproduction 8, 32, 34
reptiles 36–9
rhinoceros 24–5

S

scales 38, 39
scarlet macaw 28
sharks 6, 42–3
shortfin mako shark 43
silverback gorilla 13
silvertip shark 6
size 20, 22, 24
skeleton (insects) 44
skin 38
snakes 36, 38–9
South American spider monkeys 10
speed 24, 26, 37
spiders 6, 44
spitting cobra 39
strawberry poison frog 7

T

tails 10, 36
talons 32
tarantula 7, 44
teeth 14, 16, 20, 34, 43
tiger beetles 45
tiger shark 42
tigers 20–1
toucan 6, 29

V

venom 38, 39, 40
vertebrates 6

W

water 19, 21, 22, 26, 34–5, 40, 42
whales 26–7
white tigers 20
wings 28, 30
wolves 14–15
woolly monkey 10
worms 6

Credits

Key t=top; l=left; r=right; tl=top left; tcl=top center left; tc=top center; tcr=top center right; tr=top right; cl=center left; c=center; cr=center right; b=bottom; bl=bottom left; bcl=bottom center left; bc=bottom center; bcr=bottom center right; br=bottom right

Photos
COR=Corel Corp; DS=Digital Stock; GG=Gabrielle Green; GI=Getty Images; iS=istockphoto.com; PD=Photodisc; SH=Shutterstock

9tl GG; **11**br GI; **15**tr PD; **16**cl GI; **20**cl COR; **23**tr SH; **26**tr iS; **30**br PD; **32**tr COR; **34**bl iS; **38**tr PD; **41**cr COR; **42**tr DS; **44**cl PD

Illustrations
Front cover Ian Jackson/Kingpin br; David Kirshner c cr; Kevin Stead tr
Back cover David Kirshner tr; Tony Pyrzakowski br

Simone End **4** br, **6**c, **12**tr, **15**tr, **38**c, **40**br, **41**br; Christer Eriksson **17**br, **28**c, **33**c; Cecilia Fitzsimons/ The Art Agency **12**c; John Francis/ Bernard Thornton Artists UK **39**c; Lee Gibbons/The Art Agency **28**bl, **44**bl; Jon Gittoes **4**c, **28**c; Gino Hasler **34**c, Phil Hood/The Art Agency **14**bl, **22**t; Steve Kirk/The Art Agency **14**bl, **18**b l, **34**b; David Kirshner **3**c, **10**c, **14**c, **16**l, **41**c; Frank Knight **11**br, **21**b, **22**c, **37**bl, **38**b bl; David McAllister **30**tr; James McKinnon **8**c, **22**c, **26**bl, **30**bl, **42**b, **44**c; Colin Newman/Bernard Thornton Artists UK **24**cl, **33**br; Luis Rey/The Art Agency **12**l, **20**b bl c, **23**c, **35**c, **37**c; Peter Schouten **7**br, **8**tr, **12**l, **16**c, **43**c, **44**tr; Peter Scott/The Art Agency **19**c, **24**bl c, **40**bl, **41**br; Marco Sparaciari **31**tr; Kevin Stead **5**tr, **26**bl c, **27**tr, **30**b; Guy Troughton **1**c